Sitting Still Like a Frog

Sitting Still | Like a Still | Frog

Mindfulness Exercises for Kids
(*and Their Parents*)

ELINE SNEL

SHAMBHALA · *Boston & London* · 2013

Shambhala Publications, Inc.
Horticultural Hall
300 Massachusetts Avenue
Boston, Massachusetts 02115
www.shambhala.com

English translation © 2013 by Shambhala Publications, Inc.
Dutch edition © 2010 by Uitgeverij Ten Have
Stilzitten als een kikker: Mindfulness voor kinderen (5-12 jaar) en hun ouders
was originally published in the Netherlands by Uitgeverij Ten Have
www.uitgeverijtenhave.nl
Illustrations: Mirjam Roest

14 13 12 11 10 9
Printed in the United States of America

♾ This edition is printed on acid-free paper that meets the American
National Standards Institute Z39.48 Standard.
♻ Shambhala Publications makes every effort to print on recycled paper.
For more information please visit www.shambhala.com.

Distributed in the United States by Penguin Random House LLC
and in Canada by Random House of Canada Ltd

Page 106 constitutes a continuation of the copyright page.

In order to love you need to be at home in yourself.

I would like to thank my husband, Henk, and our children, Hans, Anne Marlijn, Koen, and Rik, for their deeply felt need to love, accept, comfort, and motivate both themselves and others at every opportunity.

Contents

Foreword

I first became aware of *Sitting Still Like a Frog* while browsing in a big bookstore in downtown Amsterdam in April 2011. It was pointed out to me by Joke Hellemanns, a Dutch Mindfulness-Based Stress Reduction teacher, who had already read it and loved it. A large stack of them was part of an even larger presentation of books on mindfulness—something that even a few years earlier would have been inconceivable in a mainstream bookstore anywhere. This prominent display was itself evidence that we are now living in a new era in which mindfulness training and practice are rapidly becoming an integral part of the landscape of life. Eline Snel's book and her work with children in Holland are part of a much larger movement that has emerged over the past ten years, in many different countries, to bring mindfulness training into schools. My first impression of Eline's book was that she was pioneering an approach that was straightforward, imaginative, and accessible to children.

The practice of mindfulness at any age is both simple and profound. Above all, it involves *learning*—learning how to cultivate greater self-awareness and greater awareness of others and the world, and then reaping the substantial benefits of that awareness, both inwardly and outwardly. The specific applications of this learning are seemingly boundless. We do not know what specific knowledge our children are going to most need ten or twenty or even five years from now because the world and their work, when they come to it, will be so different from ours. What we do know is that they will need to know how to pay attention, how to focus and concentrate, how to listen and how to learn, and how to be in wise relationship with themselves—including their thoughts and emotions—and with others. As you will see, that skill set, this approach to learning and embodied knowing, lies at the heart of mindfulness.

Mindfulness is an innate capacity that is tapped, developed, and deepened through practice. It definitely involves *cultivation*, in the sense of planting and watering seeds and then tending those seeds as they first take root and grow in the soil of our hearts and then flower and bear fruit in interesting, useful, and creative ways. It all starts with attention and being present. When the roll is called each day, children respond by saying "present." But sometimes it is only the body that is in the classroom all the same. Mindfulness is about learning to be fully present. This is exactly what this book and the guided mindfulness exercises on the enclosed CD are about.

Sitting Still Like a Frog introduces the basics of mindfulness to children in an easy-to-understand and playful way. It guides children in the cultivation of presence: presence of mind, presence of heart, and presence in the body. Presence comes when we are attentive, when we are in touch with our experience. And that quality of attentiveness is developed and deepened by paying attention to whatever is most salient and most important in each moment. This is something we are all capable of but usually don't cultivate intentionally. It requires focus and concentration. Why *not* start young in training those capacities? The world nowadays is so complex and fast-paced that knowing how to ground oneself in the present moment is an absolute necessity to make sense of the world and to continue learning, growing, and contributing what is uniquely yours to contribute in this world.

Although the cultivation of attention and awareness is called *mindfulness*, it is important to realize that it could equally well be called *heartfulness*—because it is not merely about the head and cognition, but about our entire being and our multiple intelligences and ways of knowing and being, including the cultivation of kindness toward oneself and others. Whatever we call it, studies in both medicine and neuroscience are showing that mindfulness is an essential life skill that can have profound consequences in terms of both physical and mental health. It supports and enhances learning, emotional intelligence, and overall well-being across the lifespan. This book is an excellent way for parents to learn about mindfulness and share it with their children. One of my favorite exercises, among many, is "Your Personal Weather Report."

Such training of mind and heart never used to be available to children. Now it is increasingly being brought into schools and integrated into the school day and the curriculum. Increasingly, parents also want to learn about mindfulness, both for themselves and also, perhaps, with the idea of introducing it to their children to help them get a better handle on what they might be facing in school and in life. So, helping your children learn to practice mindfulness is a worthy impulse as long as you don't inadvertently wind up foisting it on them, driven by your own expectations and enthusiasm. It is natural for us as parents to want our children to benefit from practices that train attention and emotional balance. But too much enthusiasm or too strong an attachment to a result could backfire, possibly turning our children off to mindfulness altogether. What is more, pressure of that kind is not in keeping with the non-goal-oriented essence of mindfulness practice.

This is where Eline Snel's own heartfulness and experience come into the picture. She is quite skillful when it comes to setting the right tone in which to speak to children about such matters. Her approach has a lovely playfulness to it, both for the younger children and also for preadolescents. At the same time, she takes on some of the very serious concerns that children have and helps them find creative ways to welcome and work with even their most difficult emotions and thoughts, and some of the more challenging social situations that can be such a big part of childhood. Because of its lighthearted but deeply honest perspective, *Sitting Still Like a Frog* turns the cultivation of mindfulness into something more akin to a game, an experiment, and an adventure, rather than a burden.

If the mindfulness exercises offered here and on the accompanying CD are pursued with that spirit of experimentation and adventure, they have the potential to be a huge gift to both children and parents. It will be hard *not* to pursue it in that way, because the tone of adventure and delight shines off of every page, a reflection of Eline's own compassion for children as a mother and grandmother, and her compassion for the multiple and complex stresses that school-age children these days find themselves navigating. This book, and the practices it encourages parents and children to explore together, can help buffer that stress and encourage life skills and can serve as a profound interior resource for children as they grow into adolescence and beyond.

This is doubly timely and relevant because of what is now known about the harmful effects of stress on the developing brain. Given the stress that young people are under in our society, mindfulness training is not an optional add-on to improve the learning environment or promote relaxation. It is essential for optimal learning and emotional balance, and to protect the developing brain in young people from the negative effects of excessive stress.

In adults, mindfulness training has been shown to positively influence important regions of the brain having to do with executive functioning, including impulse control and decision making, perspective taking, learning and memory, emotion regulation, and a sense of connectedness with one's own body. Under intense and unremitting stress, all these brain functions rapidly degrade. This can impair learning, wise decision making, and the development of emotional intelligence, to say nothing of self-confidence and a sense of connectedness with others. With mindfulness, these capacities become more robust. There is increasing evidence that this is even more relevant for children, whose nervous systems and brains are still in the process of developing and are even more sensitive to the negative effects of stress.

Children, of course, are naturally mindful, in the sense that they live very much in the present moment and are not so preoccupied with the past and the future. The most important thing we can do is not kill that natural quality of openness and presence but reinforce it and invite it to continue to develop. There is growing scientific evidence that mindfulness can be quite valuable to school-age children, starting even in kindergarten. Simple practices of the kind offered here can help children develop and optimize all the capacities mentioned above, as well as prosocial behaviors such as kindness, empathy, and compassion. It also helps them to put this learning to practical use in their everyday lives at home and in school.

Because mindfulness is really about attention and the awareness that arises from paying attention on purpose, in the present moment, and non-judgmentally, it is at its core universal. It does not belong to any culture or tradition or belief system. And, as we have seen, it is basic to learning anything. For this reason, and especially given the growing evidence of its efficacy in different domains, more and more teachers are seeking out training in mindfulness themselves. They, along with visionary school leaders and administrators, are leading the growing movement to bring mindfulness skills into K–12 education in appropriate ways and at appropriate levels, both in this country and abroad. In parallel with these developments, there is also a growing movement to encourage parents to bring greater mindfulness to their parenting. Both movements are being scientifically studied, and the early results are impressive.

Learning how to practice mindfulness and then bring it into all aspects of one's life as needed is similar to learning how to tune an instrument before playing it. Orchestras and musicians spend time tuning their instruments and tuning to each other. Why should we all not tune our instrument of learning before using it? Why not tune it before and during the school day, pretty much every day? What could be more basic and more important than that? What could be more important than learning and practicing how to pay attention, how to be more present, and how to be comfortable in one's own skin, with one's own thoughts and feelings and body? What could be more important than learning and practicing how to be kind to oneself and others? Aren't these lessons exactly what we most hope our children will learn? These are precisely the benefits that can flow from this book and CD.

With this in mind, I encourage parents to read through this book and practice the various meditations to get a sense of the spirit and the approach Eline offers. Next, see if one or more of your children might be interested in "playing" at exploring the CD together with you at first, using the age-appropriate practices. Then, see what happens. As noted, a light touch here is essential. You don't want to turn the practice of mindfulness into yet one more pressure on your child. Rather, it should be an opportunity for your child to tap into and befriend what is deepest and best and most unique in himself or herself and to develop those qualities in an atmosphere of openness and kindness.

May this book find its way into the hands of all the parents and children who might benefit from it. And may it bring a deep sense of self-discovery, an appreciation for one's own mind and body, and a sense of well-being and belonging.

JON KABAT-ZINN
Lexington, Mass.
April 14, 2013

Sitting Still Like a Frog

1 | Introduction to Mindfulness

At the age of five, my daughter had trouble falling asleep. Young as she was, she often asked me: "When your body wants to sleep but your head says no, how do you get to sleep?" Sometimes she would still be awake at ten. Before long she was exhausted. And so was I. She kept getting out of bed, kept awake by all the crazy thoughts that were churning around in her head: about Tim, who did not want to play with her anymore; about the goldfish floating belly-up in its bowl; about somebody under the bed who was sure to murder her. Relaxation exercises, bedtime stories, a hot bath, an irritable admonition to "go to sleep like everyone else"—nothing worked. But then I realized that if she paid less heed to the troublesome thoughts that kept popping into her head and slowly shifted her attention from her head down to her belly, she might finally calm down. There were no thoughts in her belly, only her breath, which moved her belly with its gentle rise and fall. A gentle movement. A calming movement. A movement slowly rocking her to sleep.

My daughter is twenty-one now and still does the exercise. Although simple, the exercise really helps you get out of your head and into your belly—where your thoughts cannot get to you, where all is quiet and calm.

Mindfulness—or deliberate, friendly attention—is beneficial not only for children. Parents also like to have a way to free themselves from their relentless stream of consciousness. Thoughts never stop. All you can do is stop interacting with them, stop listening to them.

This was the first mindfulness exercise that my daughter and I did together. It was the first of many. Kids like doing it just before going to sleep.

 CD EXERCISE 11, *"Sleep Tight"*

What Is Mindfulness?

Mindfulness is nothing other than present-moment awareness, an open and friendly willingness to understand what is going on in and around you. It means living in the present moment (which is not the same as *thinking about* the present moment) without judging or ignoring anything or getting carried away by the pressures of everyday life.

When you are present while waking up, while grocery shopping, with your children's sweet smiles, and with every major and minor conflict, your mind is not elsewhere but right here. You save energy, as you are aware of what is happening while it is happening. This mindful, friendly presence changes your behavior as well as your attitude toward yourself and your children.

Mindfulness is feeling the sun on your skin, feeling the salty tears rolling down your cheeks, feeling a ripple of frustration in your body. Mindfulness is experiencing both joy and misery as and when they occur, without having to do something about it or having an immediate reaction or opinion. Mindfulness is directing your friendly awareness to the here and now, at every moment. But mindfulness practice involves some effort and intentionality.

Why Mindfulness for Kids?

Mindfulness for kids meets a great need for parents and children alike to find physical and mental calm in these demanding times. But calmness alone is not enough; awareness is also needed.

Several years ago I developed a program of mindfulness training for schoolchildren. The program is called Mindfulness Matters, and it is based on Jon Kabat-Zinn's eight-week mindfulness program for adults. A total of three hundred children and twelve teachers at five schools took part in the eight-week pilots. They had a thirty-minute mindfulness session once a week and then did ten minutes of practice every day to work on what they had learned. The ten-minute sessions continued throughout the year. Both students and teachers responded with enthusiasm and noticed positive changes, such as a calmer atmosphere in the classroom, better concentration, and more openness. The kids became kinder to themselves and others, more confident, and less judgmental.

Kids are curious and inquisitive by nature. They are keen to learn things, tend to live in the moment, and can be extremely attentive. But like adults, kids are often too busy. They are tired, easily distracted, and restless. Many children do too much and have too little time to just "be." They grow up fast. Sometimes they have to juggle a dozen balls at once: socially and emotionally, at home and in school. Add to this all the things they have to learn and memorize, and it soon becomes too much. They seem to be switched on all the time, but where is the "pause" button?

By practicing mindful presence and awareness, kids learn to pause for a moment, to catch their breath, and to get a sense of what they need at this moment in time. This allows them to move out of automatic pilot mode, recognize impulses for what they are, and learn to accept that not all things in life are nice or cool. They learn to bring attention—friendly attention—to everything they do. They learn not to hide anything but instead to foster understanding of their own inner world as well as that of others.

By experiencing qualities such as attention, patience, trust, and acceptance at a young age, your children will be firmly rooted in the here and now, like saplings, with ample space to grow and be themselves.

Which Kids Benefit from Mindfulness Exercises?

Mindfulness exercises are suitable for all kids age five and up who want to calm the churning thoughts in their heads, learn to feel and understand their emotions, and improve their concentration. They also suit children who suffer from low self-esteem and need reassurance that it is okay to be themselves. A lot of kids are extremely insecure, thinking they are not good or cool enough. They worry and then deal with their distorted self-image by either withdrawing or drawing attention to themselves, by trying to please others or being selfish, or by bullying or acting tough. They become trapped in behavioral patterns that don't serve them.

The exercises are also suitable for children diagnosed with ADHD, dyslexia, and autism spectrum disorders. Of course, these exercises cannot cure disorders, but most kids really enjoy doing the exercises and also benefit from them. Mindfulness is not a form of therapy, but it can be quite therapeutic in that it can give kids a different approach to dealing with very real issues, such as an emotional storm or a compulsion to act on every impulse or thought.

Getting Started

At the back of this book you will find an audio CD with some key mindfulness exercises; they are clear and accessible, so you can get started right away. Although they are based on mindfulness training for adults, I developed the exercises especially for children and their parents. They form the core of learning to be more mindful at different times throughout the day. The book provides the framework for the exercises and helps consolidate the mindfulness practice. The exercises on the CD are all indicated by the following icon:

You can do the exercises together with your child or children. Some kids like to do the exercises on their own, and many parents love doing the exercises themselves. All the exercises lend themselves to these different approaches. You can do them sitting on a chair or a couch or lying in bed.

In addition to the exercises on the audio CD, there are also exercises in the book that you and your child can do together. You can either read the text aloud or use your own words while your child practices. Both approaches are equally effective.

Each chapter also contains some suggestions that can be put into practice any time of day: while doing the dishes, while grocery shopping, during or after dinner. They are headed "How to Do This at Home" and could provide glimpses into both your own inner world and that of your children.

How to Use the Audio CD

- Do the exercises regularly. Practice makes perfect. This applies to mindful attention just as it does to everything else. Regular practice will improve your skills. Set aside specific times for practice, perhaps a couple of times a week. Some children take to the exercises at once, while others experience resistance, thinking them boring or strange. With these children, you might ask them to agree to do an exercise five times and then ask what they make of the experience.

- Keep it lighthearted. Try to bring a playful and relaxed attitude to the exercises and have fun. If a child offers resistance, try again some other time.

- It helps to practice these exercises from time to time during the week. Your experience of the exercises changes each time you do them, and every moment is new. I recommend that you repeat the exercises on a regular basis to make the most of what they can bring you. It's an adventure of discovery.

- Be patient. Mindfulness exercises require lots of practice without being too focused on an outcome or results. It is like learning a new language or playing an instrument. A caterpillar does not turn into a butterfly overnight.
- Show appreciation when your child is practicing. Your support is essential. We all tend to be more engaged when we are encouraged.
- Ask about experiences. You can ask your children to describe their experiences after finishing an exercise. Experiences cannot be right or wrong. They are rooted in this moment. Most children like talking about them, but if they do not, then that is okay too.

2 | Parenting with Greater Mindfulness

Most parents are naturally mindful of their children at times. Still, all parents will be familiar with phrases like "Dad, you're not listening!" or "Mom, I've already told you a dozen times." Sometimes you realize you are overreacting to something your child has just said. The angry words are out before you know it, against your better judgment. Or you feel you ought to be speaking in much plainer terms: no is no, and that's that.

How is it that your reaction as a parent can be angrier, more unfriendly, or more disproportionate than intended? All of us carry old patterns from our own childhood. Some old pain may color your reaction to your thirteen-year-old son, who thinks your response when he tells you that he will come home whenever he feels like it is laughably old-fashioned: "All of my friends can decide how long they stay out." Some old fear could prevent you from articulating clearly what you really think of the situation. Obviously there is no such thing as a quick and easy recipe for being a more mindful parent. But we do have ingredients at our disposal that have traditionally led to feelings of mutual love and respect. The best-known ingredients are friendliness, understanding, openness, and acceptance. Caring touch, like a quick hug or a cuddle, is another one.

You Cannot Stop the Waves

You cannot control the sea. You cannot stop the waves, but you can learn to surf on them. This is the central idea underlying mindfulness practice. People have problems. Such is life. We all experience sadness and stress, and there are always things we simply have to deal with.

When you are really present in such situations in life, without suppressing anything or simply wishing that they weren't happening, you can see what might be needed. When you focus your attention and see the "waves" for what they really are, you can make better-informed choices and act accordingly. At such moments you become aware of your irritation as soon as it rears its head. And once you realize that you have run out of patience or that you are tempted to hit someone, you have a choice. You are then less likely to get carried away by either your own emotions or those of others. You can pause, wait, take a breather; look at the situation and note what you are feeling, thinking, or wanting to do. You become aware of the forces that whip up the waves, aware of your tendency to react automatically, and perhaps find that you are less preoccupied with how the waves "should have been."

"The Pause Button" (exercise 5 on the CD) can help. Both children and parents benefit from a breather, one just long enough to prevent an automatic reaction.

Dan is the father of two extremely rambunctious kids. He tends to react with anger whenever his kids start screaming and nagging because they cannot have it their way. "I can get furious with the eldest when he interrupts yet another important telephone conversation by begging for candy. And I feel the same with the youngest when I have rushed to pick him up from school, only to be told: 'I'm not coming with you. I'm going home with my friend John!'

"When that happens, I cannot control my anger at all. I get completely caught up in it. Within seconds we are at loggerheads. I automatically raise my voice, grab him by the arm, and tell him to do as I want. I notice that it does not make the slightest bit of

difference. In fact, I'm ashamed of my behavior, because I really want to set the right example. But I just can't do it. It's wearing us all out."

Learning to Surf

The most important step in the process of learning to surf is stopping and observing. Stopping and looking closely at the situation enables you to respond differently to difficult circumstances. Your response can then be less driven by frustration or automatic behavior and can thus be milder and more understanding. You can begin to see that it is not the situation that is causing the problems but your reaction to it. As Dan, who has benefited from the pause button, now puts it: "I still get angry sometimes, often for the same reasons. But I have learned not to react immediately and automatically. I know I have a short fuse, and I accept that, so I take a few deliberate breaths in and out before I do or say anything. It makes a world of difference."

Surfing is not an easy sport. You cannot make the waves any smaller or push them higher. They come and go at their own pace: sometimes they are high, sometimes low. Sometimes there are lots of them (a sick mother, divorced friends, imminent dismissal, and the like), and sometimes the surface of the water is smooth. By recognizing the waves in your life and not reacting immediately, you will find more peace.

Opening to Reality

I had just given birth to my son. I was twenty-five, and the smell of newborn baby filled the house like the perfume of exotic flowers. This was my first child, and it was love at first sight. The rosy cloud of motherhood was big and all-encompassing. He was so sweet and innocent. So imagine my amazement, my utter despair, when from day one my beloved boy wouldn't stop crying. He was always red with anger and wet with tears.

As soon as I put him to bed, he'd start crying his eyes out. The noise was never-ending. My anger and frustration would mount, proportionate to the amount of noise he'd make. It took every last ounce of attention and patience I could muster to resist the urge to lash out at him out of sheer powerlessness. I did not want this to be happening. I wanted to shout "Stop it!"

The prolonged crying, the fact that I never had a moment's peace, and the conclusion that I probably was not a good mother (why else would he be crying like this?) often drove me to distraction. It was only when I opened the door to my fatigue and my many doubts ("everyone can do this—everyone except me") and began to accept that I had a colicky baby that I was able to adopt a different attitude.

I could finally open up to reality: a crying baby and me as his pale, run-down young mother heading for burnout. I had no choice but to accept that the rosy cloud and the concept of the perfect mother were not reality at this point in time. Quite the opposite. It was hard work, little sleep, and a struggle to breast-feed. I was far more insecure than I thought I would be. And my baby's behavior was nowhere near as perfect as that of the ones in the parenting magazines.

As I acknowledged and accepted all of this, a weight fell from my shoulders. I stopped resisting what was happening and came to grips with what was: my crying baby needed my love just as much as a non-crying baby would. I would sniff and smell his soft skin and feel his heart beating against mine. I fell in love all over again and became better at tolerating the crying. I would rock him for hours sometimes—skin on skin in a gentle, rocking motion—until the crying eased and even stopped occasionally. Relax, breathe, surrender, let go.

A wise maternity nurse taught me to rest while rocking the baby, to nurse while I ate, to take time for myself, and to stop fighting what was happening. "Bend with the wind," was her advice, "like a young sapling." This calmed me down, calmed me right down. It enabled me to be here, in the present, with the child I loved so much.

The last things to change were my ideas about the kind of mother I had to be or the kind of child my son should have been. I decided to do my level best simply to be a mother, whatever it might take, including all the ups and downs. Mindful and curious, I met the frequent surprises head-on and increasingly cast aside my tendency to judge. I no longer demanded things to be different from the way they were, and this marked the start of a long, loving relationship in which space, respect, humor, and openness blossomed and grew into two sturdy trees, both granting each other plenty of sunlight.

And look at my son today. He is a wonderful human being and now a parent himself.

Presence, Understanding, and Acceptance

There are three fundamental qualities that have a relaxing effect on the often demanding task of parenting: presence, understanding, and acceptance. For yourself as well as for your child. Providing an open, unprejudiced perspective, these qualities enable you to see your child and yourself the way you really are and not the way you expect or wish to be (or others expect you to be). This can give your child a lifelong foundation for self-confidence, a safe nest to which she or he can return, time and time again, no matter what happens.

Presence enables you to be simply here—in contact with this moment. With these feelings and thoughts—open, curious, generous, and without an immediate opinion. Present with that small hand in yours. Present with the temper tantrum. Present with the daily school run. Present in all those moments of happiness, misfortune, routine, and everything in between. The more present you are, the less you miss. This is never a question of good or bad. Being fully present is enough.

Understanding enables you to better relate to your children and put yourself in their shoes, especially when things take an unexpected turn. Genuine interest in what is happening in your child's inner world right now can give you an insight that you did not have before. What is going on inside your child at this moment in time? What is he or she thinking about? Understanding is seeing things from your child's point of view. It's also about taking a larger view and trying to see what your child may need from you.

Acceptance is the inner willingness to recognize your child's thoughts and feelings the way you recognize your own—without wanting to change them or manipulate them, and without excluding or rejecting any aspect of either your child or yourself. Acceptance of all those moments when they fail to meet your expectations, yell when they ought to be quiet, forget to thank Grandma for her lovely present, appear to be ungrateful, or assume that you have extremely thick skin. But it is also about accepting all those moments when you are not present or kind, when you do not have the patience of a saint and you are less than an ideal parent.

Acceptance is not the same as "putting up with everything." Instead, it is the profound realization that as a parent you don't need to have an opinion on the feelings, thoughts, and actions of either your child or yourself. Acceptance originates in the profound realization that you and your children are not out for each other's blood. Even lifelong unconditional love has its ups and downs. Practicing acceptance will give you endless opportunities to open your heart and welcome *everything* that arises and work with it as mindfully as you can.

3 | Attention Starts with the Breath

B<small>EING AWARE THAT</small> you are breathing is a very powerful skill. By bringing mindful attention to your breath while you are breathing, you are present in this moment. Not in yesterday or tomorrow but in the here and now. And now is the moment that matters.

You cannot forget, leave behind, or drop your breath. You breathe for as long as you live. You are breathing right now. Can you feel it? Your breath can tell you a lot of things. It can tell you whether you are tense, calm, or restless; whether you are holding your breath or letting it flow freely.

As soon as you start observing the movement of your breath, you become more aware of your inner world, more alert to the here and now. It is also a first step toward developing concentration.

The Benefits of Attention to the Breath

When my daughter was twelve years old, she used to get upset when I told her to "just concentrate." "But I don't know how!" she would yell in frustration. "I can't do those exams; I can't concentrate, and you know it. I'm leaving school! I'm never going back."

Frustrated and angry because she kept getting distracted, she could not concentrate at all. She'd hurl her textbooks across the room. Her reaction to the chaos in her head aroused similarly strong emotions in us, her parents. Faced with such verbal onslaughts, I felt that I had failed in my duties as a parent.

I also felt tired and manipulated; I was sick of the whole thing. My many years of experience with adults and other people's children appeared to count for nothing. Nada. Zilch. Was I really always supposed to be the understanding and accepting one? Yes, of course. I am her mother. I am the one she should be able to trust without fear of rejection.

The mood was rapidly deteriorating. I had to come up with something to prevent further escalation of her emotion—and mine. At one point, following a particularly explosive outburst, she stormed upstairs to her room, slammed the door shut, and threw herself onto her bed. The silence that followed was deafening. I felt powerless. But in that silence I noticed something else, too: a vague but unmistakable desire to be with her, to be close to her and her distress, her insecurity, and her fear of failure.

I went upstairs, knocked softly on her door, and asked if I could come in. I heard some vague mumbling and entered. Reluctantly, she made some space for me on the bed. The moment had come to catch our breath—together. We were both exhausted. When I took her hand, she fell into my arms and muttered "I'm sorry, Mom," and then we cried together with relief. We must have sat like that, close to each other, for at least twenty minutes, just sitting and breathing.

At tense moments—just before an exam, for example, or a difficult conversation with a friend—children can really benefit from the power of breathing. The following story about Sara shows children how breathing can help them stay calm even when they are experiencing something quite intense. It teaches them that they need not get carried away by their reactions to "inevitable" things.

Sara, a ten-year-old girl, was on a camping vacation with her family. Having gone out with her brother to look for rabbits and deer, she fell off her bike and hit her knee on a cattle grid. Her knee was exposed to the bone.

When she heard the deafening screams, Sara's mother came running. She sensed that something was seriously wrong. When she found Sara, the girl was white as a sheet and very frightened, staring wide-eyed at the large, open wound and moaning. Shocked, Sara's mother sat down next to her daughter on the cattle grid and starting talking to her, all the while softly rubbing her back. Slowly, Sara's body began to relax.

Someone else had heard the screaming too and called an ambulance, allowing Sara's mother to carry on talking to her daughter: "I see that you've had a terrible shock, sweetheart. And it looks quite scary. But let's keep talking. How are you feeling now?" Sara said: "I think I'm going to throw up. I feel sick, and I'm scared!" She started shivering again.

"What are you most afraid of?" her mother asked.

"I'm afraid of the hospital, of having injections and surgery!"

"Well," her mother said, "we don't know what's going to happen, but whenever things are scary, one thing always works: breathing. Paying attention as you breathe in and out. It calms you down and helps you relax. And when you're relaxed, you don't feel the pain so much. It really helps."

The ambulance arrived with flashing lights, and Sara was put on a stretcher. A couple of hours later she was back at the campsite with a large white bandage around her knee. The other kids at the campground crowded around her. She had a good story for them. Her leg had not been severed, but she did have ten stitches. The kids asked her if she had been scared and whether it had hurt a lot. She replied: "Of course I was really nervous, but my mom was there with me and kept telling me to focus on my breathing. That helped." The injections and the stitches hurt, but Sara did not panic. She even watched while the doctor treated her.

Tuning in to the breath always works—for children, parents, and grandparents, and during major and minor incidents. It is the first and most important step toward a mindful response to something difficult or daunting: instead of reacting right away, you focus your attention on the breath, on a few deliberate inhalations and exhalations.

 CD EXERCISES 1, *"Sitting Still Like a Frog,"* AND 2, *"The Little Frog"*

THE ATTENTION OF A FROG

For children, practicing with the attention of a frog is an accessible way of tuning in to their breathing. I developed this frog exercise myself and do it very frequently with kids up to the age of twelve, both in school and at home. They tend to find it easy to understand and enjoyable to do.

All you need to practice sitting with the special attention of a frog is a quiet place for you and your child, a place where nobody will disturb you. It is good for other family members to know that you are "doing the frog" and do not want to be interrupted.

(Continued)

Attention Starts with the Breath |

You could introduce the exercise as follows:

"A frog is a remarkable creature. It is capable of enormous leaps, but it can also sit very, very still. Although it is aware of everything that happens in and around it, the frog tends not to react right away. The frog sits still and breathes, preserving its energy instead of getting carried away by all the ideas that keep popping into its head. The frog sits still, very still, while it breathes. Its frog tummy rises a bit and falls again. It rises and falls.

"Anything a frog can do, you can do too. All you need is mindful attention. Attention to the breath. Attention and peace and quiet."

By doing the frog exercise, children will learn to

- improve their concentration skills, which should help them to remember things better;
- be less impulsive (and not immediately act on what they are thinking or feeling);
- have some degree of control over their inner world without rejecting or repressing anything.

Sitting still with the attention of a frog is an important basic exercise.

The kids I worked with in several elementary schools did the frog exercise every day. They did it at various moments: when they had trouble concentrating, when they were sad or arguing, and sometimes just before an exam. With practice, they became better and better at it. After a while they completed their work faster and became kinder to one another. They generally liked not having to do anything for a while except sit and breathe. They calmed down and felt completely relaxed.

Tim, in kindergarten: "I like breathing and feel all soft and relaxed inside."

Thomas, in grade 6: "I never really knew what to do when my mother told me to calm down. Now I do, because I do the frog exercise every night before I go to bed."

Practicing mindful attention takes effort. It is never easy to break with habits and patterns. The same is true for our mind. By tuning in to their breath, kids learn just how easily they are distracted by thoughts, fantasies, and plans for tomorrow that pop into their heads.

All of a sudden I'm with the noise of a car outside, and I'm thinking: that must be the neighbor going to the pool. He goes every Tuesday. And then these images of my swimming lessons pop into my head, and I'm reminded of last year's vacation at the campground with the water slide.

Doing the frog on a regular basis brings you back to the here and now, to this moment, so you become aware of any distractions. As soon as you notice, you can go back to your breath or whatever else you were doing. Mindfulness is always anchored in the here and now.

How to Do This at Home

As well as doing the frog exercises on the CD, you and your family can notice your breath while watching TV or playing a computer game, at moments of tension or sadness, or when you are getting up or going to bed.

 CD EXERCISE 3, *"Attention to the Breath"*

You could ask your children to notice their breathing at the following moments:

- While watching a scary film with bated breath. Afterward you can ask them whether they noticed they were holding their breath from time to time and what this meant. You could discuss whether it might be helpful to carry on breathing during particularly tense scenes or whether the fact that they were holding their breath means the film was too scary.

- When they are completely relaxed and feeling happy and content. At such moments you could ask them how deep or shallow their breathing is, how regular or irregular. You could ask them to notice their breathing while cycling, waiting at the checkout, or chatting to a group of friends. What does their breathing tell them?

In time your children will become more and more aware of the movement of their breath—at moments of fear, sadness, relaxation, and excitement. Like a barometer, our breathing reflects our internal and external worlds.

4 | Training Your Attention Muscle

T HE SENSES PLAY a key role in the development of mindful attention. Everything you see, hear, smell, touch, and taste you perceive in this moment. You cannot smell or taste later on; it is something you do right now.

We often *think* about our sensory experiences. We judge and comment on them, saying such things as "Whenever I hear something at night, I think someone is breaking into our home." Our critical mind produces an instant and steady stream of thoughts about what we think we are seeing, hearing, tasting, smelling, and touching. And our interpretations are often far from positive. Also, our desires and expectations can have a big impact on our experience: "He must like me because he keeps looking at me."

The moment you can keep your jabbering mind at bay and use your senses without judgment, you will begin to experience the world quite differently. Unmediated reality is a wondrous thing. The more you observe reality without interference from a judging mind, the more glimpses you will catch of it. A remarkable sensation!

I Am from Mars

I did a sensory experiment with thirty-three schoolchildren age nine and ten. I asked the children to imagine that they were from Mars. This got their interest right away. You could almost hear them think, "This is going to be exciting." I asked them to close their eyes and hold up their hands so that I could give them something: two small things that every child is familiar with. This was getting even more exciting!

As soon as they felt something in their hands, they were allowed to open their eyes and look. Just look without forming an opinion. After all, they were from Mars and had no idea what they were holding in their hands.

What did they see? The two things were wrinkly, with an irregular shape.

One was almost round, the other oblong. "Brown and black at the same time," some said. What did they smell? "I can smell herbs, but I don't know what they're called." "It smells of something, but I don't know what."

Then I asked them: "What can you hear when you put them to your ear?" One of the kids said: "I can hear them squeak." Another: "I can hear a very soft scraping or something."

Then I asked them to put the things into their mouths, between their teeth, and to really taste all there is to taste when they bit into them. The classroom was quiet, except for some soft smacking noises.

One of the boys said: "I taste an explosion of sweetness in my mouth." Another student called out: "Wow, it's sweet and sour at the same time." Other kids experienced the same taste sensation.

And what was it that I put into their hands? Two small raisins. They had put them into their mouths plenty of times, but they had never tasted or seen them the way they did that day. And they had certainly never heard them squeak!

The I am from Mars exercise is an enjoyable, effective way to help kids experiment with paying attention in a new and creative way.

Open-Minded Observation

Young children are usually quite good at open-minded, inquisitive, and nonjudgmental observation. But as we grow older, we are beset with doubts and opinions. Older kids often feel insecure and think they are not good enough.

I did another observation exercise with a class of slightly older kids, sixth graders. Their task was to look carefully at twelve objects on a tray. After thirty seconds, the tray would be covered with a cloth, and the kids had to write down the objects they just saw.

One of the girls was close to panicking and said: "I can't do this, I can't remember a thing." It saddened me to see her so unsure of herself, convinced that she could not do the exercise before she had even tried. I assured her that her thoughts are not always right. She tried to concentrate, and on her first attempt she managed to remember four items from the tray—a score shared with several other kids. She was surprised.

We did the exercise with the twelve objects three times a week for two weeks. The scores increased exponentially, as did the children's self-confidence. They all remembered things better and found it easier to concentrate. And last but not least: they enjoyed it.

How to Do This at Home

Mindful attention requires practice. It does not just happen. Like playing sports or a musical instrument, you learn by practicing frequently and thoughtfully.

You can start practicing the minute you wake up. There you are:

facing a brand-new day full of things that are yet to happen. Now that you are awake, you might as well notice your legs swinging over the edge of the bed and taking you to the bathroom, where you can have a shower and feel the water's gentle caress on your skin. Waking up and realizing that you are waking up is a unique experience. You notice things that you would not normally be aware of: you notice that your body or head is still tired or that you feel well rested and fit or perhaps that you are instantly stressed out.

Mindful waking up helps you not get ahead of yourself. It grounds you in the here and now, allowing you to do things slowly before moving up a gear. If you are mindful of what you are doing while you are doing it and feel what is happening while it is happening, you are present. And when you are present in something, you learn something. Not with hindsight but right now.

LOOK BUT DON'T JUDGE

When you learn to look at things without interference from your thoughts, you will realize that you are seeing more—and interpreting less. You will also retain more, because when you look attentively, you really see things.

(Continued)

Here is an exercise for young kids:

This is a fun exercise to do on your way to school: try to remember five things that you see (a tree, a traffic sign, an unusual house, the entrance to your school, the classroom door). What do they look like? You can train yourself to see more and more properties of the tree or the traffic sign, such as colors and shapes, spots and stripes. By looking without judging whether something is pretty or ugly, you will see more of the world around you.

And for older kids:

Pick up a twig and draw it on a piece of paper. Draw exactly what you see and not what you think you are seeing. Do this a couple of days in a row and you will begin to see more and more of the twig while the drawing is becoming more and more accurate.

ARE YOU LISTENING TO ME?

It is not always easy to really listen to what is being said. Let's face it, our minds are often elsewhere and not here. But like looking, listening is something you can learn. All you need is deliberate, mindful attention and to learn to recognize its absence.

Here are some simple listening exercises:

Listening to a sound without immediately wanting to label it strengthens our ability to really listen to one another. What sounds can you hear right now? Are they high- or low-pitched, humming, or buzzing sounds? Can you detect some kind of rhythm? Are the sounds behind you or in front of you?
Far away or close? Are they outside you? Can you hear any sounds inside yourself?

Listening to one another—a fun dinnertime exercise. Everybody

(Continued)

is given two minutes to talk about his or her day or to share an important experience, while the others listen without passing judgment. Listening with a genuine desire to hear and understand what the other is saying is absolutely invaluable.

Just like you strengthen a muscle by working it, you can train your attention muscle when using all of the senses.

MINDFUL EATING

Eating with mindful attention may seem simple, but it can be quite a challenge. Try to get the whole family to eat one attentive mouthful without comments such as "*Ugh*," "Yummy," "We eat this all the time," or "I don't like this." It can be a surprising experience. Discuss what you smell, notice, taste, and feel in your mouth when you take a mindful bite, hold it in your mouth for a moment, and swallow.

Take a bite and note the following:

- What do you really taste once you stop thinking about the food's being either tasty or nasty? (Remember, these are just thoughts.)
- Do you have a salty, sweet, or bitter taste in your mouth? Or a mixture of all three?
- Does it feel hard or soft in your mouth? Rough or smooth?
- What is happening in your mouth while you are eating? What do you experience? Can you feel your mouth watering? What is your tongue doing? What happens when you swallow? And when do you lose track of your mouthful?

Mindful eating is important. When you do it, you can really taste the peanut in the peanut butter, the juiciness of the apple, the sweet softness of the banana. And another important thing: you will notice sooner when you are full.

5 | Out of Your Head and Into Your Body

W HILE ATTENTION TO your breathing and your senses gives you an immediate experience of this moment, in this chapter I will talk about awareness of the entire body. This adds yet another dimension to mindfulness practice. While I've geared the material in this chapter more toward older kids, younger children also benefit greatly from mindful awareness of the body.

Your body can tell you a great deal. Like a finely tuned instrument, it responds to emotions such as shock, tension, fear, and happiness, to cheerful thoughts or a head full of worries. These signals are all there for a reason, telling you something about your experience of this moment, about your limits and your needs. Stiff shoulders; heart palpitations; a knot in your stomach; feeling too tired to get up or the opposite, bouncing out of bed; feeling fresh and in high spirits. Your body registers it all.

While we may pick up on most of these signals, we do not always respond properly. We tend to dismiss unpleasant feelings or thoughts by passing judgment or behaving in a certain way: "Don't cry; crying is childish" or "The work needs to get done, so I'll keep going." Sometimes we simply deny the signals: "Tired? Not at all!"

The upshot is that we carry on working, pleasing others, playing games on the computer, or taking care of too much all by ourselves. And to get rid of the horrible feeling inside, we start looking for an escape—by snacking, becoming excessively rambunctious or withdrawn, or taking our negative emotions out on someone else. But these behaviors offer no real and lasting solution. The result is *double trouble:* that unpleasant feeling is now compounded by destructive and unhealthy habits.

Mindfulness teaches you how to move out of your head and into your body. By taking a brief time-out and paying attention to your body, you will notice that

- you are still angry about something that was said to you yesterday;
- you do not feel safe with a particular group of kids;
- you had far too much to eat;
- you feel incredibly energetic or tired;
- you feel sad;

- you really need to go to the bathroom, but you are not giving yourself the time.

What Is Your Body Telling You?

Most of the time your body listens to you. When you are healthy and you want to walk, your body starts walking. When you want to work or play a computer game, your body sits down at your computer. When you want to eat, your mouth opens and you chew and swallow. If you teach children to listen to their body's signals, they will learn from an early age that the body not only does what it is told but also sends out important signals that they can feel. They can feel fatigue and energy, as well as pain and the sensation of being full. They can also learn that there is no need to think about what they feel but should, rather, focus on the feeling itself—acknowledging and bringing attention to the feeling in their body is enough.

Having done this, you have a choice: What do I do with what I feel? Where do I want to take it?

I taught the following "Out of Your Head and Into Your Body" technique to a class of high school kids, and they were glad when the time came to do this exercise. They'd take off their glasses, remove their sneakers, and lie down with cushions under their heads—some on their stomachs, others on their backs. The class would breathe a collective sigh.

I asked them to be aware that they were lying down and to direct their attention to the body lying there. What was going on? What did they notice while lying there? Some noticed that they were restless or unable to relax. Others noticed that their back ached or that the floor of the sports hall was really hard or too cold.

I asked them to pay close attention to their body and to feel, from their head down to their toes, what was happening; to bring their awareness to their body without reacting or ignoring anything.

It was quiet in the class. Completely quiet. The air was filled with concentration, attention, and amazement. "One foot feels cold and the other feels warm; that's unusual," one boy said when we were sharing our experiences. Another teen commented: "I noticed that my knee hurts really badly. Weird, I hadn't noticed it before." Yet another student said: "I only just noticed that I really need to go to the bathroom." Others yawned profusely, looked a bit pale, and said they felt unbelievably tired.

A slightly older boy observed: "I've been having a lot of stomach pain recently, and now it's back." I asked him to direct some friendly attention to his stomach to see what was going on, and after a short while he said: "I feel I'm scared of getting ostracized. It's not happening to me right now, but it is to others. I'm afraid it's going to happen to me too. And I feel bad for the others, but I don't know what to do about it." This comment resulted in an open discussion about ostracism.

Limits

By listening to your body's signals, you learn more about your limits. How far can you go? How do you know?

When you do the following exercise with your children, they will experience for themselves when enough is enough. Enough is not too much, not too little, but just right.

STRETCHING AND BREATHING

Stand with your feet firmly on the floor. Throw one of your arms up in the air as high as possible and make it as long as you can. Let's see if your hand can reach the ceiling. How far can you reach? Feel how far your arm can reach while your feet remain on the floor and you carry on breathing as normal. How high can you go? There must be a limit somewhere. Where is yours? And how can you tell? Are you holding your breath? Do you think you cannot go any further? Are your muscles aching perhaps? What do you notice?

Lower your arm again. Feel how your arm is doing and

(Continued)

whether it feels any different from your other arm. What are you feeling right now? While breathing normally, throw both arms up in the air as high as possible, while your feet remain glued to the floor. Imagine some nice, juicy apples on a branch just above you. You would love to pick them, but your arms are just a bit too short to reach. They are so high up! Make your arms as long as you possibly can. And maybe even a little longer! What are you feeling in your body right now? Maybe you notice that you are holding your breath. This is one of your body's ways of telling you that you have gone far enough. Maybe your arms have started aching. Again, a signal that you have taken it far enough.

Now that you know this, you can make your arms just long enough to carry on breathing, without pain, and maybe pick an apple while you are at it. How far can you go now? Where is your limit? Can you feel it? Once you have felt your limit, slowly lower both arms again.

Looking back at the experience, what do you feel? Do your arms feel heavy or light? Do you feel a tingling sensation or something else? And how about your breathing? What do you now know about enough? And is enough always enough?

To conclude this exercise, or at a time when you feel a bit

tired, you can perk yourself up and make your skin tingle by standing where you are, cupping your hands, and rapping yourself rhythmically on the legs, buttocks, belly, chest, arms, neck, and shoulders. You finish the exercise by very gently tapping your fingers on your head, massaging your cheeks, face, and scalp. You can also do this to one another.

Every time you do these kinds of exercises with your children, you help them become a bit more aware of their body.

Limits are important. They indicate how far you can go—in eating, playing sports, teasing, or testing the rules at home. In their enthusiasm or their eagerness to get what they want, children often go on too long or take things too far, not knowing where to draw the line. This is something they need to learn from their parents, but limits can be tricky for parents too. Should a child always finish his or her meal, or not? Should you restrict your child's time playing computer games to an hour a day or let the child play as long as he or she wants? Where do you draw the line? Too much freedom is not good, but nor is an excessively authoritarian approach. It is usually best to find a happy medium, with room for negotiation and for the child to take responsibility for his or her own actions. A mother to her daughter: "I would like you to tidy your room this week. Can you do it before Saturday? Is that a deal?" But the girl would rather do it on Sunday, and that is all right too. So they reach an agreement. Firmness and flexibility combined are effective when it comes to setting limits. And so are learning to recognize when to just let things be and that what you have agreed to already is enough.

Calm Down, Relax

Some children cannot sit still for more than a few seconds, have little sense of limits, and find it difficult to calm down. Above all, they struggle to relax, taking their twitching, fidgeting, and squirming to record levels.

The youngest son of a friend of mine is an open and impulsive little guy. His big eyes are never still, his mouth never stops. His legs are constantly moving, and he is quick to bolt, like a young deer: from the table, from homework, from a game, or from a conversation on the sofa together. My friend often says with a sigh, "Calm down, will you? Relax," to which his irritated response is "It's not me who's doing the moving, it just happens!"

 CD EXERCISE 4, *"The Spaghetti Test"*

Consciously relaxing your body is different from relaxing through sports or reading. It is no better or worse, just different. Children like it when they know how to relax by doing the spaghetti test. In this test they learn how to transform stiff and uncooked pieces of spaghetti in their body into soft and supple, perfectly cooked strands of pasta. Completely limp. Totally relaxed. It helps them to recognize calm as calm and—after frequent practice—restless as restless. For the best results, kids should probably do this exercise when they are not at their most frantic, maybe just after they have watched TV or had a bath.

After the exercise, the children could try not to jump up straight-away and instead stay focused on the calmness. They could remain lying down and remain calm just a bit longer, until they notice that their body wants to start moving again—without necessarily *having* to. Without pressure. To their amazement, they will notice that calm and relaxation are nice. It gives them a bit of a break, a chance just to be.

As kids become more familiar with the different signals of their body (relaxation, restlessness, fatigue, feeling full), they are also more likely to recognize those instances when they are unwell, when they feel nauseated or in pain. We can tell our child that most of the time our bodies are healthy and do what we want them to do: walk, run, bike, play, work. But occasionally something is wrong. That is when you are ill, something you can feel.

"What is ill?" my nine-year-old son asked when suddenly, for the first time, he experienced a very strange sensation in his belly, and that is the sentiment that the following story explores:

One day Squirrel was sitting on the moss under an old tree. She wasn't feeling well. Her belly ached. Cricket happened to be passing by and noticed at once. He said: "Squirrel, you're ill."

But what exactly is ill? Squirrel wondered. She decided to ask Ant, who knew a lot about a lot of things.

"Well," Ant said, scratching her head, "there are different kinds of ill. There's a little bit ill, quite a bit ill, and very seriously ill. Seriously ill is the worst kind."

"So what happens when you're seriously ill, Ant?" Squirrel asked.

"Obviously, all kinds of things can happen, but usually nothing happens, nothing at all. After a while you just get better again."

"By the way, how's your belly?" Ant asked.

"My belly?"

"Yes."

That's when Squirrel realized that her stomachache was gone. (Based on a scene in Toon Tellegen's book Perhaps They Knew Everything*)*

After sharing this story with your young child, you could ask the child: Where do you think the stomachache went? Could there be a place where all the pain you have ever had goes? I bet there is such a place. What do you think?

HOW DO I FEEL?

- What do you notice about your body? Do you ever have stomach pains or a headache, or are you ever nauseated? When do you feel this? Would you like to talk or make a drawing about it? Does this feeling remain the same throughout the day? What can I do to help you?
- How does your body feel when you wake up? Do you feel well rested or tired?
- Copy the thermometer seven times, using one for each day of the week, and fill in the thermometer to indicate how you feel (tired at the bottom, well at the top).

LAUGHTER IS THE BEST MEDICINE

Stand in front of the mirror and start laughing. What is happening in your body? What else besides your voice is laughing? Your eyes, your cheeks, your mouth? Is your belly laughing too? And what about your shoulders? It can be great fun to do this with others.

MINDFUL WALKING

* When you run up the stairs really fast, are only your legs running? Is anything else running too? Please note exactly which muscles are getting in on the action.
* When you suddenly stop running, what do you notice about your body? What about your breathing, your muscles, your heartbeat?
* Please note how often you automatically break into a run and see if you can walk at a regular pace instead (unless you are in a great hurry or the house is on fire).

6 | Weathering the Storm Inside

Our mind is not unlike a sea or an ocean. Storms, rain showers, or the sun can transform the surface of any expanse of water into a seething mass of terrifyingly high waves or into a clear, smooth sheet through which you can see the great depths below.

The same is true for us. A particularly challenging mood or intense emotions can crop up at any time. By not wishing these feelings away or wishing they were different from what they are in the moment, you learn to notice the "weather" inside and to root yourself in what is really happening.

What Is the Weather Like Inside?

One of my children used to routinely wake up grumpy. This scenario went on for years. He would come stomping down the stairs, snorting with rage. It was hard on the steps—and on me! "I told you I didn't want anything to eat, but you put out a plate anyway." Before I'd have a chance to respond, he'd let loose again. "Where did you leave my schoolbag? You always put it in the wrong place. Now I'll be late for school, and it's all your fault!"

The back door would slam shut with a loud and ruthless bang. *Boom!*

These regular outbreaks of extremely rough inner weather eventually gave me the opportunity to recognize the first signs of an approaching storm, and I decided to try something I hadn't done before. One morning, as soon as my son came downstairs, I asked him to sit at the table. He looked at me with anger, and I noticed he was really sleepy. He didn't want to do anything, least of all sit at the table with me.

I took a few breaths and felt my shoulders bunched up with tension, but I decided to give him a friendly look anyway. I asked him again to sit down, just for a moment.

Sulking, he did as I asked, elbows on table, head clutched in hands, teeth clenched.

I asked him to observe carefully what was happening inside him.

What was he feeling right in that moment? Thunder and lightning? A storm raging? How would he grade this storm? Eight, nine, or a perfect ten? He opted for a ten before telling me in an unusually subdued voice that he was worn out. For a while now he had been pushing himself to the limit. Things were not going well in school. It was all too much. He was behind, even though he was trying really hard, and he didn't know what to do about it. His body slumped, and he gave in—gave in to that horrible feeling inside. Big tears dropped onto his breakfast. I wrapped an arm around his lanky body and just held him for a while.

Your Personal Weather Report

The personal weather report can help your child understand his or her interior world. This in turn allows you to acknowledge your child's mood and help him or her (and yourself) to accept it.

By communicating with your child and not resisting the storm, you can teach your child not to resist it either and to become aware of his or her feelings. By acknowledging awful feelings, your child will learn that it is okay to have such feelings. The two of you can then look at what is needed right at that moment: a hug, a phone call to a friend, a joint effort to find a solution to the problem, or something completely different.

As a parent this also gives you the opportunity to scrutinize your own feelings and your tendency to react automatically. Although you may not be able to solve everything, you can stay close and enable your children to express and accept their emotions. You can show them that you are on their side and that you love them, even during severe weather conditions.

YOUR PERSONAL WEATHER REPORT

Sit down comfortably somewhere, close or half close your eyes, and take some time to determine how you are feeling right now. What is the weather like inside you? Do you feel relaxed and sunny inside? Or does it feel rainy or overcast? Is there a storm raging, perhaps? What do you notice?

Without really thinking about it too much, summon the weather report that best describes your feelings at the moment. Once you know how you are doing right now, just let it be . . . just as it is . . . ; there is no need to feel or do anything differently. You cannot change the weather outside either, can you?

Stay close to this feeling for a while.

Direct your friendly and curious attention to the clouds, the clear sky, or the storm that is brewing . . . this is how it is right now . . . ; like the weather, you simply cannot change a mood. Later today the weather will be completely different again . . . , but right now this is how things are. And that is absolutely fine. Moods change. They blow over. There is no need to take any action. What a relief.

Most children enjoy this weather exercise. It makes them aware of the rain, the sun, and the storm inside them and teaches them to identify less with their moods: I am not the downpour, but I notice that it is raining; I am not a scaredy-cat, but I realize that sometimes I have this big scared feeling somewhere near my throat.

What is most important is that they allow themselves to feel the way they feel.

ACCEPTING THE WEATHER

- Draw an image that illustrates your current weather report. At the end of the day, check to see if the weather is the same or if it has changed. It helps to know that nothing ever stays exactly the same.
- On your way home from school, note the different weather conditions. Feel the rain, the cold on your cheeks, the wind that nearly blows you off your feet, the sun that warms you up. Maybe you also notice that thunderstorms either scare you or excite you.
- What mood are your parents in today? And how about your brother, sister, or friends? See if you can observe them like you would the weather outside—in a nonjudgmental way. Sometimes it rains and sometimes it is sunny. This holds true for all of us.

7 | Handling Difficult Feelings

FEELINGS ARE A RESPONSE to something you are going through, thinking, or doing. The four basic feelings are anger, sadness, fear, and happiness. Emotions can always be felt in your body. They can hit you so hard that they totally unsettle you. It is possible to get completely carried away by both pleasant and unpleasant feelings, such as love, desire, shame, insecurity, loneliness, sadness, or fear. You can feel caught right in the middle of them. More neutral feelings—such as equanimity and thoughtfulness—although less noticeable than anger or fear, exist almost like inaudible background music, and they influence your mood in subtle ways.

As soon as feelings make themselves felt in your body, they are joined by thoughts in your head. Kids attach judgments to these feelings, such as "If I show that I'm sad, they'll probably think I'm a wuss." Or they immediately register other people's thoughts about them, as in "If you're going to be angry, you'd better go to your room. I don't want to see such a face at the table."

These ideas create the impression that negative feelings are not okay and, in fact, could make your child feel that she or he is not okay. Nothing could be further from the truth. Feelings are simply feelings, and it's important that your child gets the message that "you *are not* your feelings; you *have* them." In contrast to what we often think, feelings do not last all that long. They often appear to last longer than they really do because we worry about them.

By teaching your children to admit, feel, and acknowledge feelings, you teach them something of fundamental importance. No feelings need to be suppressed, changed, or expressed immediately. It is enough to feel them and to pay friendly attention to them.

I remember one day when I was sitting at the table, preparing my classes for the next day, when my teenage daughter came home with a friend. Something was wrong. When I offered them some tea, the friend burst into tears, her skinny shoulders heaving. Her parents were getting a divorce. Haltingly, the story came out. Her father had a girlfriend. All of a sudden he was seeing someone else. The pain was intense. The hurt immense. My daughter said nothing but wrapped an arm around her friend and listened. Listened intently. She gave the story her full attention, without interrupting, without judging. She just nodded, her eyes wide with understanding. Like a wise old woman, she was supporting her friend, and I could see just how much that meant.

My daughter knew that dealing with difficult feelings is often not about solving anything, crying in sympathy, or playing the blame game—but about attention. Very loving attention.

There Is No Such Thing as a Difficult Feeling

There really is no such thing as a difficult feeling. That said, it may be difficult to handle feelings—and the resulting thoughts and behavior—especially when the feelings are big and intense. A feeling tells you something about how you experience things (not necessarily about how things really are). When it comes to handling feelings, the trick is to teach your children the following:

- They need not get carried away by their feelings or suppress anything: they can feel feelings in their body, stay with them awhile, bring attention to them, and notice that they change. Kids also benefit from putting feelings into words or drawing them: "This is pain, or this is anger; or I feel happy or betrayed, and that looks like this."

- They are not their feelings, they *have* them. "I am not a crybaby, I just happen to feel sad."
- While all feelings are okay, not all behavior is. We don't necessarily choose our feelings, but we can choose how to express them.

A mother tells me about her son, who often gets completely over-whelmed by his feelings of betrayal: "Indy has a great sense of justice. He shared a secret with a boy in his class. It was the code for an Internet game. The boy promised not to tell anyone—hand on heart. The next day in school, several more kids knew the code. When something like that happens, Indy gets distressed and angry to the point of feeling sick. He doesn't want to go to school anymore but wants to crawl into bed instead."

Nine-year-old Sofie tells me she is afraid of "just about every-thing. I'm afraid of the dark, of ghosts under the bed, of fights, of things I'm not good at. I'm afraid of walking home from school by myself."

Her eyes fill with tears and her lip quivers. When I ask her to locate the scary feelings and to feel them, she says, "I can feel them in my stomach, they're moving. Up and down and back again." I ask her to stay with this movement for a while and to pay close attention to what happens when she does. She closes her eyes and concentrates.

"It's still moving," she says, and then, "but it gets less after a while."

I ask her to stay close to this feeling for as long as possible, very tenderly and friendly. Two minutes later she opens her eyes and says, with complete surprise, "It's gone! The scary feeling is gone." She skips back to her class.

Like adults, children can be quite confused by the intensity of some feelings and often do not know how to cope. But as a parent, you can teach your children to be present with these feelings, to give these feelings their open, unprejudiced attention.

Being given such sympathetic permission to feel sadness, fear, anger, and happiness is reassuring to children. It helps them deal with the severity of the "weather" and realize that, as with a rainstorm, every feeling passes. If a feeling does get the upper hand, it can be helpful to redirect them by playing with the dog together, giving them a big hug, or holding them close. Sometimes kids want to talk about their rotten feeling. In that case, really listening is enough. But when they do not want to talk about it, all you need to do is tell them that you will be there for them if they do.

Anger Management

Anger is extremely common and can be classified as a "difficult feeling." Sometimes we may feel we shouldn't be angry. We may think that feeling angry is not okay. We may have trouble accepting the feeling, particularly if it's very intense. But there's nothing wrong with the feeling itself; it's what we do with it that can be problematic. When we're angry, we might lose control or harm others by shouting or break things and regret it later. Sometimes the anger turns inward, causing children and adults alike to hurt themselves in response to the powerlessness they feel. In all of these cases, breathing practices can help lessen the powerless or out-of-control feelings we might have.

Anger is a response to

- not getting what you want (attention, comfort, your way);
- getting what you do not want (an argument, a bad grade, tension, something you do not like eating, a missed penalty shot);
- hurt feelings (gossip, hurtful remarks such as "You're so uptight" or "You can't be on our team because you're not good enough").

I remember one spring morning negotiating with my then six-year-old daughter about what to wear to school. It was 8:25 A.M. and school was about to start. It was April, but it was cold outside. My daughter crossed her arms and looked resolute; her eyes flashed dangerously.

"I want to wear my summer coat. I'm not going to wear that stupid winter coat."

"Come on, Marlijn, or we'll be late for school," I told her.

"I'm not going to school unless I get to wear my summer coat." Her anger quickly got the better of her. She headed for the wardrobe to look for her summer coat. I managed to grab her arm, but she pulled herself free and started yelling: "I don't want to go to school" and "You're hurting me." Of course I didn't want to hurt her. Now what? School was going to start in three minutes. We'd be late.

Then I realized that she was in the grip of anger and needed my help. She could break free of it herself. I called her name, looked at her, and said: "Marlijn, I can see there's a lot of anger in you. That's fine!" I caught a glimmer of interest in her gaze. So anger is not all bad.

"Could you and your angry feeling grab your winter coat and walk to school with me?"

She nodded. We set off. The storm had blown over. We were a bit late, but that was all right. After school we would be dealing with completely different things again.

In and Out of the Maelstrom

The CD features three exercises that can help you escape the maelstrom more easily once you are in it.

When practicing with the pause button (exercise 5), children can learn to stop and take the time to note how they are doing. Looking at your inner self with curiosity and without judgment, rather than only focusing on what is happening on the "outside," can be extremely revealing. Like many parents, children have a tendency to just keep going—from school to sports, then to homework, then to sitting in front of the television—without a moment to reflect on what is going on inside. By regularly pressing the pause button, you give yourself the time and space to notice that you are breathing and to feel what is going on inside of you. And as soon as you notice, you have a choice: shall I continue with what I was doing, or do I need a short break, or do I need something else?

Exercise 6 is about noticing, experiencing, and admitting feelings. Where in your body do you feel feelings of happiness and sadness? And how do you deal with these feelings if you do not suppress or ignore them or allow them to get the better of you?

Exercise 7 offers children the chance to travel to a safe place in their own inner world—a wonderful place where they can be completely who they are.

CD EXERCISES 5, *"The Pause Button"*; 6, *"First Aid for Unpleasant Feelings"*; and 7, *"A Safe Place"*

By regularly doing these exercises with your children, you encourage them to accept feelings as they are and not to react immediately. Over time, the children will come to realize that there is no need to be afraid of the intensity of feelings. They are simply there, sometimes lingering awhile before disappearing again. In the same way that not everybody at a party is your best friend, some feelings feel much better in your body than others. But once you get to know them better, they may not be so bad and may even possess surprising qualities.

How to Do This at Home

HOW ARE YOU FEELING RIGHT NOW?

You can help your child to practice recognizing and naming all kinds of feelings as they occur. Your child can point to the picture of the frog that corresponds to his or her feelings. You can express an interest and discuss the feeling, for instance by asking the following questions:

* Where in your body do you feel it?
* How would you like to respond?

(Continued)

- Can you direct your attention to this feeling and stay with it for a while, like you might sit with your favorite pet or your friend?

Acceptance of the feeling as and when it occurs breeds recognition: "Yes, that's what anger feels like, and that's what fear feels like. Sadness feels very different again. I can direct my attention to it. It helps."

Kids also benefit from recognizing that they will "survive" intense feelings and will not be crushed by them.

It is equally important for your children to see and respect your feelings of concern, frustration, impatience, sadness, and fatigue. Sometimes you have the energy for one last game at the end of the day. "All right, but this is the very, very, very last one!" At other times you just do not feel like it. You are too tired and just want to sit and relax. And that is all right too.

8 | The Conveyor Belt of Worries

WORRYING BEGINS as soon as you want things to be other than they are right now.

I worry about not being allowed to visit my aunt. My parents have fallen out with her and now they won't let me go and see her anymore. She's my favorite aunt. My mind just keeps churning. It's giving me a headache.

I often can't sleep because I keep thinking about everything I may have done wrong. I'm often embarrassed, and then I start thinking about that too.

I often worry about my father. I don't see him a lot, because he lives in France, and that's really far away.

We worry a lot, yet we are often unaware of our worries and their connection to our thoughts, ideas, opinions, or doubts about things. We may think we can solve things by worrying, but that is a misconception. By introducing your children to the wondrous world of thoughts, you can teach them to have some influence over these thoughts. You can make the following suggestions:

- Don't believe all thoughts (the thought "I'll never manage to get a good grade" is not true).
- Realize that you *are not* your thoughts ("I'm sure I'm not nice, pretty, or funny enough").
- Jot down your top three most common worries.
- Notice these worries whenever they occur in the next couple of days, without getting caught up in them. If you observe them and don't always take them seriously, your worries can automatically extinguish, like a flame deprived of oxygen. That said, some thoughts keep coming back. These deserve special attention. They may have an underlying cause that must be examined, acknowledged, and understood before they stop nagging you.

What Are Thoughts?

Thoughts are like little voices inside your head. Like a first-class story-teller that cannot stop, this voice just keeps on talking. It interferes in everything and has an opinion about everything: about you; about the rest of the world; about your clothes; and about what you eat, do, or should have done. Thoughts are about what you find difficult or fun; about what you want to do and be or about that annoying incident last week; about the past, present, and future: everything passes along the conveyor belt of worries.

Some thoughts are about yourself: "I just cannot put tomorrow's test out of my mind and I keep thinking I'll fail."

Some are about others: "I often worry about people in other parts of the world. On the news I saw people buried under large rocks after an earthquake. That's so sad! I wish I could do something, but I don't know what." Or "That guy is such a *loser;* he looks terrible."

Thoughts and feelings tend to hang out together. They rarely see eye to eye, but they keep seeking each other out. To give an example: "I still feel sad about moving to a new house, but I think I'm being child-ish, so I won't mention it." As a parent you may be relieved because your child does not talk about the move, but because of these recurring thoughts, the sad feeling persists. And that deserves attention.

Does the Conveyor Belt Ever Stop? Can We Pause Our Thoughts?

A lot of people wonder if they can ever stop their thoughts, and it is fun to do this exercise together to try to find out. One family member keeps time for fifteen seconds. The others close their eyes and try to "think of nothing."

- Close your eyes and think of nothing for fifteen seconds.
- What do you notice? Do you keep thinking, "I'm not going to think of anything"?
- What were you thinking of?

You cannot simply stop thoughts, and there is no need to. Thoughts are produced nonstop—worries; angry thoughts; happy, fun, and naughty thoughts; ideas and plans; solutions and memories. But when these thoughts threaten to overwhelm your child, you can teach him or her to stop listening to the noise and see thoughts more like weather patterns in the mind, like passing clouds. By doing this, your child learns that he or she does not have to believe everything he or she thinks, especially since many thoughts are untrue ("I think I'm going to fail my exams"; "I think I won't be invited"; "I think I'm ugly").

Before you can work with your thoughts, you need to get to know them. What are they actually about? The following exercise can help you find out.

OBSERVING YOUR THOUGHTS

Sit down at the table with a couple of people. One person asks the questions, the others do the thinking. The interviewer asks a few questions (either the sample questions or ones he or she has made up), and the thinkers "hear" the conveyor belt of thoughts producing immediate answers in their heads. What thoughts pass by? Are they accompanied by images? You can take five seconds for each question.

* What is your favorite food?
* What makes you really happy?
* What do you worry about?
* When you give your thoughts free rein, what are they about? (take twenty seconds this time).

Thoughts are always busy. But you can choose whether to engage with them or just observe them briefly before letting them go again. It's up to you whether you believe them or simply recognize them with a smile as old friends with the habit of dropping by uninvited and telling tall tales. Once the process

(Continued)

of observing your thoughts is giving you a sense of how those thoughts are trying to steer you (toward the kitchen cupboard where the potato chips are kept as soon as you think of potato chips or toward gloominess the minute you think about the math homework you just cannot do), you begin to get a much better insight into your thinking mind.

WHAT DO YOU WORRY ABOUT?

We all worry from time to time. At such moments our mind takes us to places where doubt, fear, and lack of confidence are lurking. Sometimes your thoughts just keep on churning and keep you awake at night.

But what are they about? In order to identify the worrying thoughts, you can do the following exercise with your child and ask her or him which of the thoughts on this list make occasional or frequent appearances. Kids can jot down the corresponding thoughts in a notebook. This creates an insight into fixed patterns of thought and our habitual reactions to them.

Ask the child to complete the following thoughts, beginning with "I sometimes worry about . . . ":

- being bullied, then I think . . .
- not being good enough at things, then I think . . .
- having had an argument, then I think . . .
- someone being really mad at me, then I think . . .
- wanting to hurt others because they hurt me, then I think . . .
- whether people like me, then I think . . .
- people and animals dying, then I think . . .
- (something else), then I think . . .

It may be good to talk about the conveyor belt of worries before doing exercise 8 on the CD. Bedtime is a good time for this exercise. The head often fills with thoughts as soon as the body starts relaxing and there are no more obligations or distractions.

CD EXERCISE 8, *"The Conveyor Belt of Worries"*

FIRST AID FOR WORRIES

This exercise teaches children to shift their attention out of their head and to distance themselves from their thoughts. They can lower their attention like a small spider on a thread. Lower it farther and farther, all the way down into the abdomen. There are no thoughts inside the abdomen, only the breath—the calm movement of the breath. Deep down in the abdomen all is calm. There are no worries. There are no fights. There is peace and intense quiet.

Whenever your child is worrying, he or she need do only two things:

1. notice that he or she is worrying;
2. move out of the head and down toward the breath in the abdomen. There are no thoughts inside the abdomen.

How to Do This at Home

Here are some more strategies for calming worries:

THE LITTLE BOX OF WORRIES

For children who have difficulties doing the first aid for worries exercise and would rather do something with their hands, a nicely decorated and perhaps homemade box of worries can do the trick. Before your child turns in for the night, you can ask the child if he or she is upset about anything. Are there any worries? Things the child is getting worked up about? Thinking about these worries (instead of not thinking about them) will reveal what they are all about. These thoughts can then be put into the box. The lid comes off, the worries go in, and the lid goes back on. Your child can then look at the little box of worries somewhere on a shelf in the room—from a distance, so the child can see they are no longer in his or her head.

9 | It Is Good to Be Kind

Kindness is one of the most powerful qualities a person can possess. It is like a gentle rain that falls everywhere, without excluding a single place. It just falls without distinction. Kindness is nonjudgmental and inclusive—that is, if it is genuine. Kindness touches your heart, enabling you to grow and learn to trust yourself and others. Kindness toward yourself and others comforts, heals, and helps you to be more balanced and open, even when things are difficult or distressing.

Here's an interesting story about the healing power of kindness:

At a large university hospital pediatrics department with three specialist subwards, the young patients in one ward were responding much better to treatment than those in the others. Nobody knew why. Their clinical pictures were identical, as were their ages. Their medication was similar too.

The doctors did research but remained mystified. The difference, it turned out, is explained by human kindness. On the one ward a Surinamese cleaning woman went around mopping the floors every day. As she passed the children's beds, she sang Surinamese lullabies, took the time to listen to stories and questions, and lovingly ruffled the young patients' hair. Her warmth, joy, and unconditional love helped the kids there recover faster than on the other wards.

Most often, children are close to their kind nature. Trusting and a bit dreamy or restless, they take each day as it comes, happy with the way things are. But there are exceptions. For example, an eight-year-old boy named Sander came to see me in my practice with symptoms of anxiety and insomnia. His parents told me that he was being bullied at school—not very openly but in an underhanded and undermining way. It all started with a deflated bicycle tire. No one knew who was responsible. Then Sander's coat got moved so that he could no longer find it. Again, the culprit was nowhere to be found. And then small groups of boys surrounded him after school, mocking him and calling him names. Sander was afraid to go home by himself. He was feeling helpless, vulnerable, and alone. He kept thinking it was his own fault, which only added to the insecurity.

Fortunately, Sander confided in his parents. They sought help when their son had trouble sleeping at night and taught him to stand up for himself and take charge of the situation. This may not have reduced the bullying immediately, but it helped him feel like less of a victim. He started taking judo lessons, and while remaining the friendly guy he always was, he now responds more assertively when the other boys start threatening him.

Is It Worth Fighting Back?

Would hitting back or bullying and name-calling in return be a more effective approach? Some think so, but I disagree. Ultimately, physical and verbal abuse will only provoke more aggression, more antagonism, and further trouble. But what you can do is show that you are not weak or a pushover.

As we saw in Sander's story, there are other ways of dealing with a sense of intimidation. There is no need to walk away or start fighting, but you can still make it clear, either verbally or physically, that you will not be pushed around.

Once upon a time, somewhere on this earth, there was a snake who was fed up with people screaming and running away from him. He went into the forest and asked a wise old man who lived there what he could do to make people fear him less. The sage gave it some thought and said: "You could try not to hiss or show your venomous fangs and pretend to be completely harmless."

The snake decided to give it a try, but the strategy backfired. As soon as the villagers realized that they were no longer in danger, they started pelting the poor creature with large rocks. The snake narrowly escaped with his life and writhed back to the wise old man. Now what?

The man sent the snake back, telling him to show his mighty fangs and flex his muscles but not to squirt venom and injure people. This time around, the villagers kept a respectful distance, sensing the snake's might as it slowly slithered into the village. Nothing happened, but everybody knew it was a distinct possibility.

Kindness Is a Skill

While practicing kindness during the Mindfulness Matters lessons in school, the children learned to reflect on people who are particularly considerate and nice to them, to recognize what love feels like. Many mothers and fathers, stepmothers and stepfathers, grandpas and grandmas got a mention during the exercise. Next up, the kids learned that they can send the same stream of warm, loving feelings to others, even to a parent or a grandparent who is no longer alive.

You can send friendly thoughts and wish others to be happy wherever they are, at any time, whenever you feel like it. You can even send them to yourself.

Practicing kindness enables children to recalibrate their heart's compass. The final lessons of Mindfulness Matters are about compassion.

A tough little preschool child with spiky hair and a mischievous look in his eyes expressed his surprise after doing the compassion exercise: "I notice that lots of people love me, but" —and he jabbed a finger at his chest— "I don't think I'm very nice. I can be really naughty!" Suddenly he looked extremely small and vulnerable.

Kids learn that being unkind every now and then is not the end of the world (we all get moody or say harsh things from time to time), but being aware that you are unkind when you are sheds some light on your own behavior and gives you more freedom of action. It brings each child a step closer to compassion, to a better world of his or her own making. It is good to be kind. For everyone, kids included.

In another lesson, there were twenty-eight preadolescents practicing kindness in a school sports hall. Not a single child thought it was strange. Dead serious, they stood in a big circle around a beautiful soft "compliment ball."

The first kid picked up the ball, called out the name of a class-mate, and said, while throwing the ball to him, "I think it's amazing that after a fight you're always the first one to try and make it up again." "Thanks," the recipient said, and reflected a moment before throwing the ball to a girl across from him and saying: "I like you because you're always yourself. You're never silly or anything." As she accepted the ball and the compliment, a shy smile broke through. She passed the ball on with the message: "You're special because you're a real friend. You're such a good listener."

I was touched when I saw the ball going to a boy who is a bit of a bully and troublemaker in class. He was given the ball with the words "I think you're so much nicer than last year."

Following these exercises, the teachers noticed changes in the class-room. During a meeting, they expressed their surprise. "They're giving each other a lot more space." "I often hear them saying it's 'cool' and 'great' when someone has done something he thought was difficult. The mood has really changed. They're helping each other, and there are fewer cliques."

CD EXERCISES 9, *"A Little Boost,"* and 10, *"The Secret of the Heart Chamber"*

"A Little Boost" and "The Secret of the Heart Chamber" will enhance awareness of and reflection on enjoyable moments.

How to Do This at Home

We all like a compliment. It is priceless to hear someone tell you that you are good and that you are loved just the way you are. It is also nice to hear *what* the other person likes about you. It is the kind of thing you are likely to remember years later. Like precious jewels, sincere compliments and kind remarks are cherished and stored—in the chamber of the heart.

NOTICING YOUR UNKINDNESS

You and your family can make bracelets out of elastic bands. This bracelet is worn on your right wrist, for weeks if need be, as a reminder to be nice to yourself and others. Whenever you think you are acting thoughtlessly, being unkind to yourself or genuinely unpleasant toward others, you move the bracelet to your other wrist. As soon as it happens again, you move the

(Continued)

bracelet back. This makes you more aware of every act of un-kindness. And instead of telling yourself off when it happens, you just move the bracelet to your other wrist with a smile on your face. Please note: others should not interfere in this process by pointing out your failures or unkindness. You do it for yourself.

This exercise is not about telling you that you cannot be un-kind. It is about noticing that you are unkind. And as soon as you notice, you have a choice: do you stick with it or do you stop, now that you know?

LOOKING AT THE BIGGER PICTURE

Look for someone close to you (at home or in school) who both-ers you a lot, someone you dislike or would rather avoid. Now spend the day, secretly, without anyone else knowing, looking for tenderness, generosity, kindness, or any other positive trait in this person. He or she need not become your best friend, but it is good to see that someone is not just unkind.

I LIKE YOU BECAUSE . . .

The following exercise can be done with all family members who can write, including Grandpa and Grandma. The results can be kept forever. Kindness does not fade, and love never falters; they keep touching your heart.

Everybody is given a piece of paper with the names of all family members and relatives. Take your time to call to mind what you appreciate about the others. Then, after every name, you write one sweet, nice, or unforgettable thing about that person. Fold the paper and hand it to your mom or dad, who then keeps the notes.

A few weeks later, he or she takes them all out again to compile lists of the compliments made about each person. One day everybody will find his or her personal list under the pillow.

It is heartwarming to read what you do not often hear. It is touching to realize how nice and sweet you really are, without having to make a special effort—just by being you. Precisely for being you.

10 | Patience, Trust, and Letting Go

I F ONLY WE HAD the patience of a caterpillar in a cocoon, waiting to transform into a butterfly. If only we had the trust of a newborn child. Or if only we could let go with the wisdom of a leaf in the fall. Our lives would surely be easier. There are so many things we wish were different: better, safer, prettier, easier, or back to the way they used to be. Disappointment, sadness, wanting to be less lonely, or not seeing any light at the end of the tunnel—these are feelings that we all have from time to time. At such moments, desire kicks in, a deep-seated wish for things to be different from the way they are now. Wishes and desires are important. In fact, they are the first step toward a better world, a safer place, good health. Wishes and desires are healthy but difficult too.

They keep drawing attention to what you do not have rather than what you do have. How do you handle them without becoming "trapped" by what you badly want but do not have?

What Is the Desire Really About?

As a parent you can be aware of an immense desire in your child. A desire for something to stop (being bullied, a row with a friend, an illness, those horrible pimples, getting fat) or for an achievement (a good exam result, a successful classroom presentation, more confidence). In many instances these desires can be realized through action: hard work, frequent practice, a better diet, doing difficult sums. But what about desires outside your field of influence, such as recovering from a nasty illness or your child's desire to spend more time on his or her birthday with the child's father, who lives in a distant town?

Some situations simply cannot be changed, not even with the best will in the world, because it is just the way things are. So is there absolutely nothing you can do about an extremely strong desire for a happy ending or a change in the situation?

Luckily, there is! You can always change your attitude toward the situation, and visions can help you with this. Not nightmare visions but dream visions.

Your Inner Movie Theater

We all have the ability to see pictures inside our heads with our eyes closed. Sometimes these are just some random, unconnected pictures. Sometimes they are entire movies, making you feel as if you were in an inner movie theater with someone else at the controls, switching the movies on and off again. You "see" a creepy guy climbing through your window in the dead of night, or you "see" yourself repeatedly failing an important exam.

We are responsible for generating all of these images, often unconsciously and habitually. In and of themselves, these images have no value other than the one you attach to them. But if your mind can produce scary pictures (nightmare visions), can it also generate nice pictures (dream visions)? Yes: by deliberately tapping into this particular skill of your mind, you can create beautiful and enjoyable pictures, just like a real film director.

A six-year-old girl receives a bike for her birthday. Much to her parents' surprise, she hops on and cycles off, effortlessly. When asked how she learned to do this so quickly, she says: "I kept picturing how to do it. In my mind I saw myself cycling."

When Saskia, who is in eighth grade, gave a presentation, she did much better than on previous occasions. Shortly before the presentation, she had done the sitting still like a frog exercise, which helped her relax. And she spent the weeks leading up to the presentation picturing herself facing the class, relaxed, steady, and brimming with self-confidence. It took only two minutes a day.

By deliberately mobilizing internal images, you can uncover hidden qualities. Such images are not meant to compensate for something, act like a magic wand, or achieve the impossible. They merely visualize something that is already in you and that you want to reinforce, improve, or rely on—like an artist who can see the potential of a block of rough stone in her mind's eye expresses her vision by steadily chipping away at the material.

Picturing Your Heart's Desire

When I ask children about their heart's desire, I get to hear poignant stories about great and frequently well-hidden desires. They often think about them in bed but rarely discuss them, convinced that the situation is hopeless anyway or afraid to cause their already beleaguered parents further pain.

My mother tells me I must to learn live with the fact that I'm ill and won't get better, but I don't know how!

I want my parents to talk to each other again. They're divorced and haven't spoken properly for almost a year.

I don't want to be sick anymore. I just want to be like any other child.

I really miss my granddad—I wish he wasn't dead.

Even in the face of such seemingly unattainable desires, images can be effectively mobilized—not out of a wish to manipulate reality but out of the wisdom and knowledge that sooner or later things will change. Sometimes your attitude toward the situation changes, sometimes it's the situation itself that changes. There is usually no way of knowing in advance. But a change will come. It always does. The following exercise can help.

THE WISHING TREE ·

A beautiful old visualization technique introduces children to the process of patience, trust, and letting go. It helps them visualize their desires, teaching them to have faith in change and encouraging them to let go—to let go of the desire to control, to let

(Continued)

go of things they cannot influence. Eventually they will realize that once they stop obsessing about it, a change is more likely to come.

Sit up straight and comfortably. You can close or half close your eyes. Sitting like this, you can tune in to your breathing. Tuning in to your breathing is always special. It brings you here, to where you are sitting right now. In this very spot. Hold your attention on your breath for a while. Take your time to feel the familiar movement of the breath. The breath goes in and out . . . in and out again.

When you are ready, you can come along to a beautiful place in nature. Maybe it is a place you have visited before or maybe it's an imagined place . . . take your time to look around and see where you are. It is nice and quiet in this place. Safe and pleasant and with great views. What do you see?

If you look into the distance, you will see an old tree. Why don't you walk over to it? It is a beautiful old tree, a very special tree. It is a wishing tree that has stood there for more than a century. The tree is large and solid. It has a beautiful thick trunk and wide branches with bright green leaves. Look closely and you will see white doves sitting on the branches of the tree. Some are close together, others keep to themselves. There are quite a few.

Each dove can fulfill one of your heart's desires. Not immediately, but when the time is ripe. And not just any wish but wishes that come straight from the heart and are truly important to you.

Now take your time to let a wish surface of its own accord, straight from the heart. There is no need to think, just wait for something to come up. It can be a feeling or an idea too. It can be something you have never talked to anyone about. What is coming up?

As soon as you know, you call out softly, without anyone else hearing, for one of the doves. Let it sit on your hand, and then hold your hand close to your heart. Tell the dove your heart's deepest desire. It will understand. Give your wish to the dove and release the bird. Let it go. Watch the dove fly off, farther and farther away—on its way to fulfill your heart's desire. Not today or tomorrow. And maybe not next week either. But rest assured that things will change. Not always exactly the way you wanted it, maybe not quite as fast as you were hoping, but often even better than expected. One day you will notice a change, maybe when you have stopped thinking about it. Have faith. Have faith and let go of the wish and all the accompanying images.

Calmly, open your eyes again and remain seated for a while.

It is important to discuss the wishing tree meditation with your child. Ask about the child's experiences and accept whatever he or she is prepared to say about them.

An eleven-year-old girl talks of missing her mother, who has passed away. During the wishing tree meditation, the girl expresses the strong desire to see her again. I ask her where she feels it when she thinks of her mother. The girl's face softens and she looks really sweet when she says: "I feel her in my heart."

"Can you see her when you think of her?"

"A little bit, in a small halo of light."

I tell her that she can direct her attention to her heart to see her mother, every day, as often as she likes. Maybe she would like to do a drawing of her mother inside her heart?

Three weeks later she proudly shows me the drawing. It hangs above her bed. The horrible feeling of loss has turned into something else. Acceptance. Every day, just before going to bed, she talks to her mother. And suddenly she likes her father's new girlfriend a little bit more too.

A girl who was being bullied in school told her mother about the wishing tree. Her deepest wish was not to be bullied anymore.

The mother had not known about the bullying, but now she sprang into action. She visited the school to discuss the matter. The school responded positively by setting up a meeting with the girl, the bully, and the homeroom teacher. The bullying did not happen again. That is how quickly a wish can come true.

Patience, trust, and letting go play an important role in all desires, big and small. Patience, because there is a time for everything. Trust, because you know there will always be change. And, finally, letting go, because you have to let go of the need to manipulate and control this process, let go of the idea that things have to be done your way. This process of letting go of control, in particular, is never easy, but remember: letting go is not the same as giving up.

We are inclined to think that surrendering control equals giving up our desire for change and putting up with the way things are. Nothing could be further from the truth. Acceptance in the sense of acknowledgment actually opens doors. It is liberating to understand that change does not necessarily stem from *wanting* something different, from manipulating, expecting, or even demanding change, but from *knowing* that something *will* be different. Come what may. It gives you the freedom to choose how to deal with everything that happens in the lives of both you and your children, regardless of the force and height of the waves, just as the little boy discovered in the following story.

Once upon a time there was a boy who longed to become a surfer. But he was only ten, lived too far from the sea, and had no money to buy a board. He still dreamed about it though. Night and day. With his eyes closed, he could see himself surfing the waves. He could even feel it. He could smell the sea and feel the tension in his muscles. Concentrating really hard and continually shifting his balance, he imagined himself riding the waves. It was really exciting. He managed to pull it off more and more often. Now. This wave is mine. This very wave. Wow! This is it. This is great. But would he ever be able to surf for real?

One day he and his parents set off on vacation. They were going to the Côte Sauvage, in Brittany, France. He had no idea where that was, but after a ten-hour drive, they arrived at their destination, feeling hot and tired. As soon as he got out of the car, he smelled the sea. Thrilled, he ran to the beach, and what he saw there in the evening light was amazing. Several boys were lying in a group in the water. Like young walruses, they were waiting for the right wave. As soon as a beautiful wave rose up, they quickly paddled over and leaped on their boards to catch the wave. One of the boys surfed toward the beach and yelled: "You want to try? It's really cool. Have you done it before?"

The boy said timidly: "No, never, but I'd love to try."

The surfer handed over his board. It was a nice white one with a small blue dolphin on the bottom. The boy grabbed the board, determined to give it a go. He paddled through the powerful surf with some difficulty, as he had done so often in his imagination. At the sight of the first high wave, he stood up, planting his feet firmly on the board. He held his breath. Would he be okay? Yes, he was okay. He was doing great. This is what he had dreamed of. This is what he used to see when he closed his eyes and thought of surfing. And now his dreams were coming true. Of course, he still had a lot to learn. It did not always come as easily as that first time, but because he really wanted to surf, he got better and better at it.

This boy is now a well-known surfing instructor in Scheveningen, on the Dutch coast, where he teaches hundreds of children. He teaches them trust and letting go as well as surfing. Trust that the right moment will come along. This moment. Trust that the next wave will always come along and to let go of the idea that the waves ought to be moving exactly the way we want them to.

Surfing the waves of life gives you insight not only into your own nature but also into the ever-changing natural world of which you are a part.

Good luck with the exercises and may they help you and your children to live even more mindful, relaxed, and confident lives.

Acknowledgments

With patience, openness, and absolute faith, Wim and Willy van Dijk, Henk Jansen, Jolan Douwes, Leo Bras, and Bea van Burghsteden of the NIS schools' association in Amersfoort, the KPOA (Foundation for Catholic Elementary Education), three hundred pupils, and the teachers and boards of several schools in Amersfoort and Leusden, the Netherlands, lent me their support, offered me positive feedback, and persuaded me to write this book. *Sitting Still Like a Frog* touched their hearts. The frog itself owes its unique appearance to Mirjam Roest.

My children and grandchildren are a daily source of inspiration to me. Time and time again they teach me that nothing about the process of growing up can be taken for granted—and that love conquers all.

My husband reads every single line that I write, with infinite patience, an open mind, and natural wisdom. His constructive criticism always simplifies, clarifies, and improves my writing. I am grateful for our close relationship and our unique spiritual equality.

I would also like to thank my editor Beth Frankl at Shambhala Publications. Her knowledge and advice proved to be absolutely invaluable. Myla and Jon Kabat-Zinn have been an immense support to me in the production of the English-language edition of this book. It was Jon who, on the recommendation of my colleague Joke Hellemans, took the Dutch book to the United States, and Myla who kindly agreed to record the CD. Their commitment, belief, ever-present kindness, and assistance with the translation of the text made this English-language edition possible. Both on a personal level and in my role as a mindfulness trainer, it has been a privilege to work with Myla and Jon. Inspiring and unforgettable.

Thank you, thank you all so much for your help.

Bibliography

Ferrucci, Piero. *What We May Be: The Vision and Techniques of Psychosynthesis.* New York: Aquarius, 1990.

Fontana, David, and Ingrid Slack. *Meditating with Children: A Practical Guide to the Use and Benefits of Meditation Techniques.* Rockport, Mass.: Element Books, 1997.

Judith, Anodea. *Wheels of Life: The Classic Guide to the Chakra System.* Woodbury, Minn.: Llewellyn Publications, 1987.

Kabat-Zinn, Jon. *Full Catastrophe Living: Using the Wisdom of Your Body and Mind to Face Stress, Pain, and Illness.* New York: Delta, 1990.

Kabat-Zinn, Jon, and Myla Kabat-Zinn. *Everyday Blessings: The Inner Work of Mindful Parenting.* New York: Hyperion, 1998.

Kornfield, Jack. *The Wise Heart: A Guide to the Universal Teachings of Buddhist Psychology.* New York: Bantam Dell, 2009.

About the Author

Eline Snel (b. 1954) has been working as an independent therapist since 1980. For more than twenty years she has been developing meditation and mindfulness training programs. In 2004 she began to teach eight-week mindfulness courses for adults, parents, and children, as well as educators and health care professionals. Eline is the founder and owner of the Academy for Mindful Teaching (AMT) in Leusden, Netherlands, where she and her colleagues teach the AMT children's trainer course. The course offers professionals the opportunity to teach the mindfulness training program Mindfulness Matters to kids and teens ages four to nineteen. Eline also teaches the program in Belgium, France, and Germany. More information is available at www.academyformindful teaching.com and www.elinesnel.nl. For children's training by AMT instructors, see www.aandachtwerkt.com.

CD Exercises

1. *Sitting Still Like a Frog*
Basic meditation for kids age 7–12

2. *The Little Frog*
Basic meditation for kids age 5–12 or anyone who
wants a simpler, shorter version of exercise 1

3. *Attention to the Breath*
Directing and shifting your attention
For kids age 7–12 and older

4. *The Spaghetti Test*
Relaxation for kids age 5–12 and older

5. *The Pause Button*
How not to react automatically
For kids age 7–12 and older

6. *First Aid for Unpleasant Feelings*
For kids age 7–12 and older

7. *A Safe Place*
Visualization for kids of all ages

8. *The Conveyor Belt of Worries*
When those thoughts won't stop churning
For kids age 7–12 and older

9. *A Little Boost*
When things are looking down
For kids age 5–12

10. *The Secret of the Heart Chamber*
Practicing kindness
For kids age 7–12

11. *Sleep Tight*
For kids of all ages

Library of Congress Cataloging-in-Publication Data

Snel, Eline.
[Stilzitten als een kikker. English]
Sitting still like a frog: mindfulness exercises for kids
(and their parents) / Eline Snel.—First edition.
Pages   cm
Translation of the author's Stilzitten als een kikker.
Includes bibliographical references.
ISBN 978-1-61180-058-6 (pbk.: alk. paper)
1. Mind and body. 2. Awareness. 3. Child psychology. 4. Consciousness. I. Title.
BF161.S63613 2013
155.4'13—dc23
2013004159